Mornings with
Henri J.M. Nouwen

READINGS AND REFLECTIONS

COMPILED BY

EVELYN BENCE

SERVANT
BOOKS

PUBLISHED BY ST. ANTHONY MESSENGER PRESS
CINCINNATI, OHIO

Selections from *Clowning in Rome* by Henri J. M. Nouwen. © 1979 by Henri J. M. Nouwen. Used by permission of Doubleday, a division of Bantam Doubleday Dell Publishing Group, Inc. From *Creative Ministry* by Henri J. M. Nouwen. © 1971 by Henri J. M. Nouwen. Used by permission of Doubleday, a division of Bantam Doubleday Dell Publishing Group, Inc. From *A Cry for Mercy* by Henri J. M. Nouwen. © 1981 by Henri J. M. Nouwen. Used by permission of Doubleday, a division of Bantam Doubleday Dell Publishing Group, Inc. From *The Genesee Diary* by Henri J. M. Nouwen. © 1976 by Henri J. M. Nouwen. Used by permission of Doubleday, a division of Bantam Doubleday Dell Publishing Group, Inc. From *The Inner Voice of Love* by Henri Nouwen. © 1996 by Henri Nouwen. Used by permission of Doubleday, a division of Bantam Doubleday Dell Publishing Group, Inc. From *Reaching Out* by Henri Nouwen. © 1975 by Henri J. M. Nouwen. Used by permission of Doubleday, a division of Bantam Doubleday Dell Publishing Group, Inc. From *The Return of the Prodigal Son* by Henri Nouwen. © 1992 by Henri J. M. Nouwen. Used by permission of Doubleday, a division of Bantam Doubleday Dell Publishing Group, Inc. From *The Wounded Healer* by Henri J. M. Nouwen. © 1972 by Henri J. M. Nouwen. Used by permission of Doubleday, a division of Bantam Doubleday Dell Publishing Group, Inc.

LIBRARY OF CONGRESS CATALOGING-IN-PUBLICATION DATA

Nouwen, Henri J. M.
Mornings with Henri J.M. Nouwen : readings and reflections.
   p.   cm.
Includes bibliographical references.
ISBN 0-86716-674-6
1. Spiritual life–Catholic Church–Meditations.   I. Title.
BX2182.2.N669   1997
242'.2–dc21   97-36041
                                     CIP

Cover photograph © 1996 by Neal McDonough. Used by permission.

ISBN-13: 978-0-86716-674-3
ISBN-10: 0-86716-674-6

Published by Servant Books, an imprint of St. Anthony Messenger Press
28 W. Liberty St.
Cincinnati, OH 45202
www.ServantBooks.org
Printed in the United States of America.

08 09 10 11 6 5 4 3

Introduction

Henri Nouwen was one of the most popular and profound spiritual writers of our time.

A priest, psychologist and famed professor, Nouwen is remembered as being "one of us." Struggling to reconcile the paradoxes inherent in life and the Christian faith. Searching to find his heart's true home. Celebrating the unexpected epiphanies that bring joy and delight.

As he aged, his style changed. A young pastoral voice relaying "shoulds" and "oughts" turned personal, drawing readers into his life—the joy and the sorrow—as if they were his circle of friends. Readers who had never met him mourned his sudden death in 1996.

I trust these selections introduce new readers to Nouwen and his take on themes that defined his life: prayer, solitude, and community. And in later writings he hammered hard on variations of one particular theme: the unlimited love of God.

Other readers, who are Nouwen enthusiasts, might find here a compact refresher, insights that will challenge their walk, lighten their load, and draw them close to Christ and to the memory of an old friend.

If you like this book, pick up any of the books cited in the acknowledgments in the back of the book. Discover the wealth of wisdom penned by this fellow traveler.

Evelyn Bence

1
As Time Goes By

Lord, life passes by swiftly. Events that a few years ago kept me totally preoccupied have now become vague memories; conflicts that a few months ago seemed so crucial in my life now seem futile and hardly worth the energy; inner turmoil that robbed me of my sleep only a few weeks ago has now become a strange emotion of the past; books that filled me with amazement a few days ago now do not seem as important; thoughts which kept my mind captive only a few hours ago, have now lost their power and have been replaced by others.

Why is it so hard to learn from this insight? Why am I continuously trapped by a sense of urgency and emergency? Why do I not see that you are eternal, that your kingdom lasts forever, and that for you a thousand years are like one day? O Lord, let me enter into your presence and there taste the eternal, timeless, everlasting love with which you invite me to let go of my time-bound anxieties, fears, preoccupations, and worries. "Seek first the Kingdom," you said, "and all these other things will be given you as well." All that is timebound will show its real meaning when I can look at it from the place where you want me to be, the place of undying love.

2
What We Are Called to Do . . .

It is not easy to distinguish between doing what we are called to do and doing what we want to do. Our many wants can easily distract us from our true action. True action leads us to the fulfillment of our vocation. Whether we work in an office, travel the world, write books or make films, care for the poor, offer leadership, or fulfill unspectacular tasks, the question is not "What do I most want?" but "What is my vocation?" The most prestigious position in society can be an expression of obedience to our call as well as a sign of our refusal to hear that call, and the least prestigious position, too, can be a response to our vocation as well as a way to avoid it ....

When we are committed to do God's will and not our own we soon discover that much of what we do doesn't need to be done by us. What we are called to do are actions that bring us true joy and peace ....

Actions that lead to overwork, exhaustion, and burnout can't praise and glorify God. What God calls us to do we *can* do and do *well*. When we listen in silence to God's voice and speak with our friends in trust we will know what we are called to do and we will do it with a grateful heart.

3
Reflect on the Meaning

When a child is born, friends get married, a parent dies, people revolt, or a nation starves, it's not enough just to know about these things and to celebrate, grieve, or respond as best we can. We have to keep asking ourselves: "What does it all mean? What is God trying to tell us? How are we called to live in the midst of all this?" Without such questions our lives become numb and flat.

But are there any answers? There are, but we will never find them unless we are willing to live the questions first and trust that, as Rilke says, we will, without even noticing it, grow into the answer. When we keep the Bible and our spiritual books in one hand and the newspaper in the other, we will always discover new questions, but we also will discover a way to live them faithfully, trusting that gradually the answer will be revealed to us.

4
Reclaimed Memories

All of ministry rests on the conviction that nothing, absolutely nothing, in our lives is outside the realm of God's judgment and mercy. By hiding parts of our story, not only from our own consciousness but also from God's eye, we claim a divine role for ourselves; we become judges of our own past and limit mercy to our own fears. Thus we disconnect ourselves not only from our own suffering but also from God's suffering for us. The challenge of ministry is to help people in very concrete situations—people with illnesses or in grief, people with physical or mental handicaps, people suffering from poverty and oppression, people caught in the complex networks of secular or religious institutions—to see and experience their story as part of God's ongoing redemptive work in the world. These insights and experiences heal precisely because they restore the broken connection between the world and God and create a new unity in which memories that formerly seemed only destructive are now reclaimed as part of a redemptive event.

5
Right and Light

Dear Lord, you say, "Shoulder my yoke and learn from me, for I am gentle and humble in heart." These words stayed with me today because I realized how often I complain about my yoke and hear others complain about theirs. So often I consider life and its many tasks and concerns burdensome, and then it does not take much to become pessimistic or depressed, to ask for attention to my "unique" problem, and to spend much time and energy in expressing annoyance and irritation.

You do not say, "I will take your burden away," but, "I invite you to take on my burden!" Your burden is a real burden. It is the burden of all human sin and failings. You carried that burden and died under its weight. Thus you made it into a light burden.

O Lord, turn my attention from the false burden to the real burden, and let me carry your burden in union with you. I know that only then will I be able to overcome the temptations of bitterness and resentfulness, and live joyfully and gratefully in your service.

Let me better understand your words, "My yoke is easy and my burden light." Amen.

6
Listen to the Blessing

For me personally, prayer becomes more and more a way to listen to the blessing ....

Often you will feel that nothing happens in your prayer. You say: "I am just sitting there and getting distracted." But if you develop the discipline of spending one half-hour a day listening to the voice of love, you will gradually discover that something is happening of which you were not even conscious. It might be only in retrospect that you discover the voice that blesses you. You thought that what happened during your time of listening was nothing more than a lot of confusion, but then you discover yourself looking forward to your quiet time and missing it when you can't have it. The movement of God's Spirit is very gentle, very soft—and hidden. It does not seek attention. But that movement is also very persistent, strong and deep. It changes our hearts radically.

7
Invited to Enter the Intimacy

This week I often experienced resistance toward private prayer. Every time I tried to sit down and pray alone my thoughts wandered to the book I was reading and wanted to continue reading, to my feelings of hunger, to a monk I couldn't figure out, to a hostile feeling or a daydream I couldn't shake off. Usually I ended up reading a few minutes trying to focus my thoughts again. But when I knelt in front of the Icon of Our Lady of Vladimir, it was different. In some way my resistance against meditation subsided, and I simply enjoyed being invited to enter into the intimacy between Jesus and Mary.

[Abbot] John Eudes didn't run away from the psychological implications of all this. He made me see how masculine my emotional life really is, how competition and rivalry are central in my inner life, and how underdeveloped my feminine side had remained …. John Eudes also reminded me that the Hebrew word for God's Spirit, *Ruach,* is both masculine and feminine, and thus emphasizes that God is male and female. Mary helps me to come in touch again with my receptive, contemplative side and to counterbalance my one-sided aggressive, hostile, domineering, competitive side.

8
Turning Thoughts into Conversation

To pray, I think, does not mean to think about God in contrast to thinking about other things, or to spend time with God instead of spending time with other people. Rather, it means to think and live in the presence of God. As soon as we begin to divide our thoughts into thoughts about God and thoughts about people and events, we remove God from our daily life and put him in a pious little niche where we can think pious thoughts and experience pious feelings. Although it is important and even indispensable for the spiritual life to set apart time for God and God alone, prayer can only become unceasing prayer when all our thoughts—beautiful or ugly, high or low, proud or shameful, sorrowful or joyful—can be thought in the presence of God. Thus, converting our unceasing thinking into unceasing prayer moves us from a self-centered monologue to a God-centered dialogue. This requires that we turn all our thoughts into conversation. The main question, therefore, is not so much what we think, but to whom we present our thoughts.

9
Revolutionary Prayer

When you pray, you open yourself to the influence of the Power which has revealed itself as Love. The Power gives you freedom and independence. Once touched by this Power, you are no longer swayed back and forth by the countless opinions, ideas and feelings which flow through you. You have found a center for your life that gives you a creative distance so that everything you see, hear and feel can be tested against the source. Christ is the man who in the most revealing way made clear that prayer means sharing in the power of God. It enabled him to turn his world around, it gave him the attraction to draw countless numbers out of the chains of their existence, but it also stirred up aggression which brought him to his death. Christ, who is called the Son of Man and also the Son of God, has shown what it means to pray. In him, God himself became visible for the fall and rise of many.

Prayer is a revolutionary matter because once you begin, you put your entire life in the balance. If you really set about praying, that is, truly enter into the reality of the unseen, you must realize that you are daring to express a most fundamental criticism, a criticism which many are waiting for, but which will be too much for many others.

10
The Paradox of Prayer

The same saints and spiritual guides, who speak about the discipline of prayer, also keep reminding us that prayer is a gift of God. They say that we cannot truly pray by ourselves, but that it is God's spirit who prays in us. St. Paul put it very clearly: "No one can say, 'Jesus is Lord' unless he is under the influence of the Holy Spirit" (1 Cor 12:3). We cannot force God into a relationship. God comes to us on his own initiative, and no discipline, effort, or ascetic practice can make him come. All mystics stress with an impressive unanimity that prayer is "grace," that is, a free gift from God, to which we can only respond with gratitude. But they hasten to add that this precious gift indeed is within our reach. In Jesus Christ, God has entered into our lives in the most intimate way, so that we could enter into his life through the Spirit ….

So, the paradox of prayer is that it asks for a serious effort while it can only be received as a gift. We cannot plan, organize or manipulate God; but without a careful discipline, we cannot receive him either. This paradox of prayer forces us to look beyond the limits of our mortal existence.

11
This Is Possible Only If ...

This discipline of prayer embraces many forms of prayer—communal as well as individual prayer, oral as well as mental prayer. It is of primary importance that we strive for prayer with the understanding that it is an explicit way of being with God. We often say, "All of life should be lived in gratitude," but this is only possible if at certain times we give thanks in a very concrete and visible way. We often say, "All our days should be lived for the glory of God," but this is only possible if a day is regularly set apart to give glory to God. We often say, "We should love one another always," but this is only possible if we regularly perform concrete and unambiguous acts of love. Similarly, it is also true that we can only say, "All our thoughts should be prayer," if there are times in which we make God our only thought.

12
When We Live with Hope

When we live with hope we do not get tangled up with concerns for how our wishes will be fulfilled. So, too, our prayers are not directed toward the gift, but toward the one who gives it. Our prayers might still contain just as many desires, but ultimately it is not a question of having a wish come true but of expressing an unlimited faith in the giver of all good things. You wish that ... but you hope for.... For the prayer of hope, it is essential that there are no guarantees asked, no conditions posed, and no proofs demanded, only that you expect everything from the other without binding him in any way. Hope is based on the premise that the other gives only what is good. Hope includes an openness by which you wait for the other to make his loving promise come true, even though you never know when, where or how this might happen.

13
The Paradox of Expectation

The paradox of expectation indeed is that those who believe in tomorrow can better live today, that those who expect joy to come out of sadness can discover the beginnings of a new life in the center of the old, that those who look forward to the returning Lord can discover him already in their midst.

You know how a letter can change your day. When you watch people in front of the wall of mailboxes, you can see how a small piece of paper can change the expression on a face, can make a curved back straight, and a sullen mouth whistle again....

A life lived in expectation is like a life in which we have received a letter, a letter which makes him whom we have missed so much return even earlier than we could imagine. Expectation brings joy to the center of our sadness and the loved one to the heart of our longings. The one who stayed with us in the past and will return to us in the future becomes present to us in that precious moment in which memory and hope touch each other.

14
The Mother of Expectation

The mother of expectation is patience.... Patience comes from the word "patior" which means to suffer.

Joy and sadness are as close to each other as the splendid colored leaves of a New England fall to the soberness of the barren trees. When you touch the hand of a returning friend, you already know that he will have to leave you again. When you are moved by the quiet vastness of a sun-covered ocean, you miss the friend who cannot see the same. Joy and sadness are born at the same time, both arising from such deep places in your heart that you can't find words to capture your complex emotions.

But this intimate experience in which every bit of life is touched by a bit of death can point us beyond the limits of our existence. It can do so by making us look forward in expectation to the day when our hearts will be filled with perfect joy, a joy that no one shall take away from us.

15
Torn Between Two Worlds

The great spiritual task facing me is to so fully trust that I belong to God that I can be free in the world—free to speak even when my words are not received; free to act even when my actions are criticized, ridiculed, or considered useless; free also to receive love from people and to be grateful for all the signs of God's presence in the world. I am convinced that I will truly be able to love the world when I fully believe that I am loved far beyond its boundaries.

When I awoke from my operation and realized that I was not yet in God's house but still alive in the world, I had an immediate perception of being sent: sent to make the all-embracing love of the Father known to people who hunger and thirst for love.

16
The Paradox of Grace

All the beauty of Mary comes from Jesus, yet she is so completely her own. All the sanctity of Bernadette is given to her by Jesus yet she owns every part of herself with complete freedom. All that there is of love in me is a gift from Jesus, yet every gesture of love I am able to make will be recognized as uniquely mine. That's the paradox of grace. The fullest gift of grace brings with it the fullest gift of freedom. There is nothing good in me that does not come from God, through Christ, but all the good in me is uniquely my own. The deeper my intimacy with Jesus, the more complete is my freedom.

Whatever I am to be in the years ahead, anything that may be good about it comes from Jesus. But what comes from Jesus I can truly claim as most fully my own.

17
Dealing with Duality

There is within you a lamb and a lion. Spiritual maturity is the ability to let lamb and lion lie down together. Your lion is your adult, aggressive self. It is your initiative-taking and decision-making self. But there is also your fearful, vulnerable lamb, the part of you that needs affection, support, affirmation, and nurturing.

When you heed only your lion, you will find yourself overextended and exhausted. When you take notice only of your lamb you will easily become a victim of your need for other people's attention. The art of spiritual living is to fully claim both your lion and your lamb. Then you can act assertively without denying your own needs. And you can ask for affection and care without betraying your talent to offer leadership.

Developing your identity as a child of God in no way means giving up your responsibilities. Likewise, claiming your adult self in no way means that you cannot become increasingly a child of God. In fact, the opposite is true. The more you can feel safe as a child of God, the freer you will be to claim your mission in the world as a responsible human being. And the more you claim that you have a unique task to fulfill for God, the more open you will be to letting your deepest need be met.

18
Beloved of God

The greatest gift my friendship can give to you is the gift of your Belovedness. I can give that gift only insofar as I have claimed it for myself. Isn't that what friendship is all about: giving to each other the gift of our Belovedness?

Yes, there is that voice, the voice that speaks from above and from within and that whispers softly or declares loudly: "You are my Beloved, on you my favor rests." It certainly is not easy to hear that voice in a world filled with voices that shout: "You are no good, you are ugly; you are worthless...."

These negative voices are so loud and so persistent that it is easy to believe them. That's the great trap. It is the trap of self-rejection.

19
Blessed to Bless

The blessed one always blesses. And people want to be blessed! This is so apparent wherever you go. No one is brought to life through curses, gossip, accusations or blaming. There is so much of that taking place around us all the time. And it calls forth only darkness, destruction and death. As the "blessed ones," we can walk through this world and offer blessings. It doesn't require much effort. It flows naturally from our hearts. When we hear within ourselves the voice calling us by name and blessing us, the darkness no longer distracts us. The voice that calls us the Beloved will give us words to bless others and reveal to them that they are no less blessed than we.

20
Your Heart Is Only Love

Lord, how can I ever go anywhere else but to you to find the love I so desire! How can I expect from people as sinful as myself a love that can touch me in the most hidden corners of my being? Who can wash me clean as you do and give me food and drink as you do? Who wants me to be so close, so intimate and so safe as you do? O Lord, your love is not an intangible love, a love that remains words and thoughts. No, Lord, your love is a love that comes from your human heart. It is a heart-felt love that expresses itself through your whole being. You speak ... you look ... you touch ... you give me food. Yes, you make your love a love that reaches all the senses of my body and holds me as a mother holds her child, embraces me as a father embraces his son and touches me as a brother touches his sister and brother.

O dear Jesus, your heart is only love. I see you; I hear you; I touch you. With all my being, I know that you love me.

21
Catch the Vision

God not only says: "You are my Beloved." God also asks: "Do you love me?" and offers us countless chances to say "Yes." That is the spiritual life: the chance to say "Yes" to our inner truth. The spiritual life, thus understood, radically changes everything. Being born and growing up, leaving home and finding a career, being praised and being rejected, walking and resting, praying and playing, becoming ill and being healed—yes, living and dying—they all become expressions of that divine question: "Do you love me?" And at every point of the journey there is the choice to say "Yes" and the choice to say "No."

Once you are able to catch a glimpse of this spiritual vision, you can see how the many distinctions that are so central in our daily living lose their meaning. When joy and pain are both opportunities to say "Yes" to our divine childhood, then they are more alike than they are different.

22
The Question Shifts

That God reveals the fullness of divine love first of all in community, and that the proclamation of the good news finds its main source there has radical consequences for our lives. Because now the question is no longer: *How can I best develop my spiritual life and share it with others?* but *Where do we find the community of faith to which the Spirit of God descends and from which God's message of hope and love can be brought as a light into the world?* Once this question becomes our main concern we can no longer separate the spiritual life from life in community, belonging to God from belonging to each other and seeing Christ from seeing one another in him.

23
The Mystery of Love

Without the solitude of heart, our relationships with others easily become needy and greedy, sticky and clinging, dependent and sentimental, exploitative and parasitic, because without the solitude of heart we cannot experience the others as different from ourselves but only as people who can be used for the fulfillment of our own, often hidden, needs.

The mystery of love is that it protects and respects the aloneness of the other and creates the free space where he can convert his loneliness into a solitude that can be shared. In this solitude we can strengthen each other by mutual respect, by careful consideration of each other's individuality, by an obedient distance from each other's privacy and by a reverent understanding of the sacredness of the human heart. In this solitude we encourage each other to enter into the silence of our innermost being and discover there the voice that calls us beyond the limits of human togetherness to a new communion. In this solitude we can slowly become aware of a presence of him who embraces friends and lovers and offers us the freedom to love each other, because he loved us first (see 1 Jn 4:19).

24
The Memory of My Present Joy

Surrounded by a loving, supportive community, Advent and Christmas seem pure joy. But let me not forget my lonely moments because it does not take much to make that loneliness reappear. If I am able to remember loneliness during joy, I might be able in the future to remember joy during loneliness and so be stronger to face it and help others face it. In 1970 I felt so lonely that I could not give; now I feel so joyful that giving seems easy. I hope that the day will come when the memory of my present joy will give me the strength to keep giving even when loneliness gnaws at my heart. When Jesus was loneliest, he gave most. That realization should help to deepen my commitment to service and let my desire to give become independent of my actual experience of joy. Only a deepening of my life in Christ will make that possible.

25
Only Half the Story

In Bolivia the Advent symbols are different from those I am used to. In the past, Advent always meant to me the shortening of days, the approach of winter, and the time in which nature became darker and colder until the day of light. But now I have to learn to wait for the coming of the Lord while spring becomes summer and the light increases day by day. Now Advent means the coming of hot days with their fertile showers. Now Advent is the time during which schools are closed and children play on the streets. Now Advent means a time of blossoming trees and first fruits. And so the symbols of Easter become symbols of Christmas. Maybe my first Advent in the southern part of our planet will reveal to me new things about the mystery of God's becoming flesh among us. Until now, nature has only told me half of the story of God's incarnation; now the other half can be told.

But I have to listen, quietly, patiently, and with inner expectation. Nature can only tell me its other half of the story when I am ready to hear it, when my heart is not so full of false images and unnecessary preoccupations that there is no place left to receive the good news I have not yet heard.

26
Make My Fear a Prayer

Today, O Lord, I felt intense fear. My whole being seemed to be invaded by fear. No peace, no rest; just plain fear: fear of mental breakdown, fear of living the wrong life, fear of rejection and condemnation, and fear of you. O Lord, why is it so hard to overcome my fear? Why is it so hard to let your love banish my fear? Only when I worked with my hands for a while did it seem that the intensity of the fear decreased.

I feel so powerless to overcome this fear. Maybe it is your way of asking me to experience some solidarity with the fearful people all over the world: those who are hungry and cold in this harsh winter, those who are threatened by unexpected guerrilla attacks, and those who are hidden in prisons, mental institutions, and hospitals. O Lord, this world is full of fear. Make my fear into a prayer for the fearful. Let that prayer lift up the hearts of others. Perhaps then my darkness can become light for others, and my inner pain a source of healing for others.

You, O Lord, have also known fear.… Make my fear, O Lord, part of yours, so that it will lead me not to darkness but to the light.

27
Know That You Are Welcome

Not being welcome is your greatest fear. It connects with your birth fear, your fear of not being welcome in this life, and your death fear, your fear of not being welcome in the life after this. It is the deep-seated fear that it would have been better if you had not lived.

Here you are facing the core of the spiritual battle. Are you going to give in to the forces of darkness that say you are not welcome in this life, or can you trust the voice of the One who came not to condemn you but to set you free from fear? You have to choose for life. At every moment you have to decide to trust the voice that says, "I love you. I knit you together in your mother's womb" (Ps 139:13).

Everything Jesus is saying to you can be summarized in the words "Know that you are welcome." Jesus offers you his own most intimate life with the Father.

28
Not "Where?" or "What?" But "How?"

Today, I realized that the question of where to live and what to do is really insignificant compared to the question of how to keep the eyes of my heart focused on the Lord. I can be teaching at Yale, working in the bakery at the Genesee Abbey, or walking around with poor children in Peru and feel totally useless, miserable, and depressed in all these situations. I am sure of it, because it has happened. There is not such a thing as the right place or the right job. I can be happy and unhappy in all situations. I am sure of it, because I have been. I have felt distraught and joyful in situations of abundance as well as poverty, in situations of popularity and anonymity, in situations of success and failure. The difference was never based on the situation itself, but always on my state of mind and heart. When I knew that I was walking with the Lord, I always felt happy and at peace. When I was entangled in my own complaints and emotional needs, I always felt restless and divided.

It is a simple truth that comes to me in a time when I have to decide about my future. Coming to Lima or not for five, ten, or twenty years is no great decision. Turning fully, unconditionally, and without fear to the Lord *is*.

29
A Mother's Dying Agony

What then is this agony? Is it fear of God, fear of punishment, fear of the immensity of the divine presence? I do not know, but if I have any sense of what I saw, it was more profound. It was the fear of the great abyss which separates God from us, a distance which can only be bridged by faith. The test comes when everything that is dear to us slips away ... and there is absolutely nothing left to hold on to. It is then that one must have the faith to surrender to a loving Lord, to believe that he will not allow us to fall into a cruel and bottomless canyon, but will bring us to the safe home which he has prepared for us. My mother knew her weaknesses and shortcomings. Her long life of deep prayer had not only revealed to her God's greatness, but also her own smallness; not only God's openheartedness, but also her own fearfulness; not only God's grace, but also her own sinfulness. It seemed that it was precisely her lifelong conversation with God that made her death such an agonizing event. At the hour of death all becomes faith. Faith in God, who knows every fiber of our being and loves us in spite of our sins, is the narrow gate which connects this world with the next.

30
A Family's Deathbed Prayers

As we found ourselves gathered around mother's bed, our prayer was easy, free, spontaneous and natural. It offered us words of greater power and meaning than any of the words we could have said to one another. It gave us a sense of unity which could not be created by speculations on the nature of mother's illness or her chances of recovery. It provided a sense of togetherness that was more given than made, and it created a place in which we could rest together.

Some of the prayers we said were ones that mother had taught us as children, prayers that now came to mind again after years of absence. Some were prayers which had never been spoken before, while others were prayers which have been repeated over the centuries by men and women in pain and agony.

The prayers we said together became the place where we could be together without fear or apprehension. They became like a safe house in which we could dwell, communicating things to each other without having to grope for inadequate, self-made expressions. The psalms, the Our Father, the Hail Mary, the Creed … and many other prayers formed the walls of this new house, a safe structure in which we felt free to move closer to each other and to mother, who needed our prayers in her lonely struggle.

31
Signs of Hope

Perhaps the main task of the minister is to prevent people from suffering for the wrong reasons. Many people suffer because of the false supposition on which they have based their lives. That supposition is that there should be no fear or loneliness, no confusion or doubt. But these sufferings can only be dealt with creatively when they are understood as wounds integral to our human condition. Therefore ministry is a very confronting service. It does not allow people to live with illusions of immortality and wholeness. It keeps reminding others that they are mortal and broken, but also that with the recognition of this condition, liberation starts.

No minister can save anyone. He can only offer himself as a guide to fearful people. Yet, paradoxically, it is precisely in this guidance that the first signs of hope become visible. This is so because a shared pain is no longer paralyzing but mobilizing, when understood as a way to liberation. When we become aware that we do not have to escape our pains, but that we can mobilize them into a common search for life, those very pains are transformed from expressions of despair into signs of hope.

32
The Older Brother's Complaint

Whenever I express my complaints in the hope of evoking pity and receiving the satisfaction I so much desire, the result is always the opposite of what I tried to get. A complainer is hard to live with, and very few people know how to respond to the complaints made by a self-rejecting person....

Once, when I felt quite lonely, I asked a friend to go out with me. Although he replied that he didn't have time, I found him just a little later at a mutual friend's house where a party was going on. Seeing me, he said, "Welcome, join us, good to see you." But my anger was so great at not being told about the party that I couldn't stay. All of my inner complaints about not being accepted, liked, and loved surged up in me, and I left the room, slamming the door behind me. I was completely incapacitated—unable to receive and participate in the joy that was there. In an instant, the joy in that room had become a source of resentment.

This experience of not being able to enter into joy is the experience of a resentful heart. The elder son [in the parable of the Prodigal Son] couldn't enter into the house and share his father's joy. His inner complaint paralyzed him and let the darkness engulf him.

33
Free to Give and Live and Die

I was hit by a car and soon found myself in a hospital close to death. There I suddenly had the illuminating insight that I would not be free to die as long I was still holding on to the complaint of not having been loved enough by the one whose son I am. I realized that I had not yet grown up completely. I felt strongly the call to lay to rest my adolescent complaints and to give up the lie that I am less loved than my younger brothers. It was frightening, but very liberating. When my dad, far advanced in years, flew over from Holland to visit me, I knew that this was the moment to claim my own God-given sonship. For the first time in my life, I told my father explicitly that I loved him and was grateful for his love for me…. As I look back on this spiritual event, I see it as a true return, the return from a false dependence on a human father who cannot give me all I need to a true dependence on the divine Father who says: "You are with me always, and all I have is yours"; the return also from my complaining, comparing, resentful self to my true self that is free to give and receive love.

34
Like the Prodigal, Choose Life

Judas betrayed Jesus. Peter denied him. Both were lost children. Judas, no longer able to hold on to the truth that he remained God's child, hanged himself. In terms of the Prodigal Son, he sold the sword of his sonship. Peter, in the midst of his despair, claimed it and returned with many tears. Judas chose death. Peter chose life. I realize that this choice is always before me. Constantly I am tempted to wallow in my own lostness.... There are always countless events and situations that I can single out to convince myself and others that my life is just not worth living, that I am only a burden, a problem, a source of conflict, or an exploiter of other people's time and energy. Many people live with this dark, inner sense of themselves. In contrast to the prodigal, they let the darkness absorb them so completely that there is no light left to turn toward and return to. They might not kill themselves physically, but spiritually they are no longer alive. They have given up faith in their original goodness and, thus, also in their Father who has given them their humanity.

But when God created man and woman in his own image, he saw that "it was very good," and, despite the dark voices, no man or woman can ever change that.

35
Mary Calls Me Back

I am discovering in my own life as a priest that without Mary I cannot fully enter into the mystery of Jesus' compassionate love. It is hard to explain why this is so, but I see now, mostly retrospectively, how I used to speak more about Jesus than to him. Most of all, I see now how Jesus had become more an argument for the moral life than the door to the mystical life which is the life in communion with God, Father, Son and Holy Spirit. Mary calls me back to where I most want to be: to the heart of God which, as you know, is also the heart of the world. She calls me to let the passion of Jesus become my passion and his glory become my glory. She calls me to move beyond the dos and don'ts of the morally correct life into an intimacy with God where I can live the sadness, pain and anguish of this world while already tasting the gladness, joy and peace of the glorified Lord.

Mary didn't just call *me* to that life. She also invites *you* to that same life. That is why with great urgency I ask you to go to Mary and learn from her how to live in this anguishing world as peace-bringing witnesses of her Son.

36
The Simpler My Heart, The More Clearly I See

The risen Jesus is not bound to any place or person. He is totally free. Simplicity and freedom belong together. Purity too. I realize that I need not be at Lourdes to find peace and joy. Lourdes simply reminds me that purity, simplicity and freedom belong to the heart and can be lived anywhere.

Mary met Jesus after the Resurrection, but not as he was met by Mary of Magdala or John or Peter or the disciples on the road to Emmaus. She didn't need to be convinced of anything. Her heart was so simple, so pure, so free that her encounter with her risen Son could be completely interior. A heart that truly knows Jesus doesn't need an apparition. Jesus and Mary were always present to each other in sorrow and joy. I know now that the purer and simpler my heart is, the more clearly I will see—wherever I am.

37
The Secret of Waiting

The secret of waiting is the faith that the seed has been planted, that something has begun. Active waiting means to be present fully to the moment, in the conviction that something is happening where you are that you want to be present to it. A waiting person is someone who is present to the moment, who believes that this moment is the moment.

A waiting person is a patient person. The word "patience" means the willingness to stay where we are and live the situation out to the full in the belief that something hidden there will manifest itself to us.

38
Being Present in the Present

Celebrating is first of all the full affirmation of our present condition. We say with full consciousness: We are, we are here, we are now, and let it be that way. We can only really celebrate when we are present in the present. If anything has become clear, it is that we have to a large extent lost the capability to live in the present. Many so-called celebrations are not much more than a painful moment between bothersome preparations and boring after-talks. We can only celebrate if there is something present that can be celebrated. We cannot celebrate Christmas when there is nothing new born here and now, we cannot celebrate Easter when no new life becomes visible, we cannot celebrate Pentecost when there is no Spirit whatsoever to celebrate. Celebration is the recognition that something is there and needs to be made visible so that we can all say Yes to it.

39
The Mystery of Life

The mystery of life is that the Lord of life cannot be known except in and through the act of living. Without the concrete and specific involvements of daily life we cannot come to know the loving presence of him who holds us in the palm of his hand. Our limited acts of love reveal to us his unlimited love. Our small gestures of care reveal his boundless care. Our fearful and hesitant words reveal his fearless and guiding Word. It is indeed through our broken, vulnerable, mortal ways of being that the healing power of the eternal God becomes visible to us. Therefore, we are called each day to present to our Lord the whole of our lives—our joys as well as sorrows, our successes as well as failures, our hopes as well as fears. We are called to do so with our limited means, our stuttering words and halting expressions. In this way, we will come to know in mind and heart the unceasing prayer of God's Spirit in us. Our many prayers are in fact confessions of our inability to pray. But they are confessions that enable us to perceive the merciful presence of God.

40
The New Reality of Marriage

When two people commit themselves to live their lives together, a new reality comes into existence. "They become one flesh," Jesus says. That means that their unity creates a new sacred place. Many relationships are like interlocking fingers. Two people cling to each other as two hands interlocked in fear. They connect because they cannot survive individually. But as they interlock they also realize that they cannot take away each other's loneliness. And it is then that friction arises and tension increases. Often a breakup is the final result.

But God calls man and woman into a different relationship. It is a relationship that looks like two hands that fold in an act of prayer. The fingertips touch, but the hands can create a space, like a little tent. Such a space is the space created by love, not by fear.

41
Nature as a Sacramental Pointer

I remember sitting day after day at the same table in a dull restaurant where I had to eat my lunch. There was a beautiful red rose in a small vase in the middle of the table. I looked at the rose with sympathy and enjoyed its beauty. Every day I talked with my rose. But then I became suspicious. Because while my mood was changing during the week from happy to sad, from disappointed to angry, from energetic to apathetic, my rose was always the same. And moved by my suspicion I lifted my fingers to the rose and touched it. It was a plastic thing. I was deeply offended and never went back there to eat.

We cannot talk with plastic nature because it cannot tell us the real story about life and death. But if we are sensitive to the voice of nature, we might be able to hear sounds from a world where man and nature both find their shape. We will never fully understand the meaning of the sacramental signs of bread and wine when they do not make us realize that the whole of nature is a sacrament pointing to a reality far beyond itself.

42
Be Surprised by Joy

There is suffering ahead of us, immense suffering, a suffering that will continue to tempt us to think that we have chosen the wrong road and that others were more shrewd than we. But don't be surprised by pain. Be surprised by joy, be surprised by the little flower that shows its beauty in the midst of a barren desert, and be surprised by the immense healing power that keeps bursting forth like springs of fresh water from the depth of our pain.

And so, with an eye focused on the poor, a heart trusting that we will get what we need, and a spirit always surprised by joy, we will be truly powerful and walk through this valley of darkness performing miracles because it's God's power that will go out from us.

43
Lord of Our Minds

Do we really want our mind to become the garbage can of the world? Do we want our mind to be filled with things that confuse us, excite us, depress us, arouse us, repulse us, or attract us whether we think it is good for us or not? Do we want to let others decide what enters into our mind and determines our thoughts and feelings?

Clearly we do not, but it requires real discipline to let God and not the world be the Lord of our mind. But that asks of us not just to be gentle as doves, but also cunning as serpents! Therefore spiritual reading is such a helpful discipline. Is there a book we are presently reading, a book that we have selected because it nurtures our mind and brings us closer to God?... Even if we were to read for only fifteen minutes a day in such a book, we would soon find our mind becoming less of a garbage can and more of a vase filled with good thoughts.

44
Confessing Idolatry

This withholding from God of a large part of our thoughts leads us onto a road that we probably would never consciously want to take. It is the road of idolatry. Idolatry means the worship of false images, and that is precisely what happens when we keep our fantasies, worries, and joys to ourselves and do not present them to him who is our Lord. By refusing to share these thoughts, we limit his lordship and erect little altars to the mental images we do not want to submit to a divine conversation.

I vividly remember how I once visited a psychiatrist to complain about my difficulty in controlling my fantasy life. I told him that disturbing images kept coming up and that I found it hard to detach myself from them. When he had listened to my story, he smiled and said, "Well, Father, as a priest you should know that this is idolatry, because your God is saying that you should not worship false images." Only then did I realize fully what it really means to confess having sinned not only in word and action but also in thought. It means confessing idolatry, one of the oldest and most pervasive temptations.

45
Beyond Entertainment

Radio, television, newspapers, books, films, but also hard work and a busy social life all can be ways to run away from ourselves and turn life into a long entertainment.

The word *entertainment* is important here. It means literally "to keep (*tain* from the Latin *tenere*) someone in between (*enter*)." Entertainment is everything that gets and keeps our mind away from things that are hard to face. Entertainment keeps us distracted, excited, or in suspense. Entertainment is often good for us. It gives us an evening or a day off from our worries and fears. But when we start living life as entertainment, we lose touch with our souls and become little more than spectators in a lifelong show. Even very useful and relevant work can become a way of forgetting who we really are. It is no surprise that for many people retirement is a fearful prospect. Who are we when there is nothing to keep us busy?

Silence is the discipline that helps us to go beyond the entertainment quality of our lives. There we can let our sorrows and joys emerge from their hidden place and look us in the face, saying: "Don't be afraid; you can look at your own journey, its dark and light sides, and discover your way to freedom."

46
Celebrating Life

Birthdays need to be celebrated. I think it is more important to celebrate a birthday than a successful exam, a promotion, or a victory. Because to celebrate a birthday means to say to someone: "Thank you for being you." Celebrating a birthday is exalting life and being glad for it. On a birthday we do not say: "Thanks for what you did, or said, or accomplished." No, we say: "Thank you for being born and being among us."

On birthdays we celebrate the present. We do not complain about what happened or speculate about what will happen, but we lift someone up and let everyone say: "We love you."

47
Table Talk

When, on the evening before his death, Jesus came together with his disciples around the table, he revealed both intimacy and distance. He shared the bread and the cup as a sign of friendship, but he also said, "Look, here with me on the table is the hand of the man who is betraying me."

When I think about my own youth, I think most often of our family meals, especially on feast days. I remember the Christmas decorations, the birthday cakes, the Easter candles, and the smiling faces. But I also remember the words of anger, the walking away, the tears, the embarrassment, and the seemingly endless silences.

We are most vulnerable when we sleep or eat together. Bed and table are the two places of intimacy. Also the two places of greatest pain. And, maybe, of these two places, the table is the most important because it is the place where all who belong to the household gather and where family, community, friendship, hospitality, and true generosity can be expressed and made real.

48
An Awesome Love

True love between two human beings puts you more in touch with your deepest self. It is a love in God. The pain you experience from the death or absence of the person you love, then, always calls you to a deeper knowledge of God's love. God's love is all the love you need, and it reveals to you the love of God in the other. So the God in you can speak to the God in the other. This is deep speaking to deep, a mutuality in the heart of God, who embraces both of you.

Death or absence does not end or even diminish the love of God that brought you to the other person. It calls you to take a new step into the mystery of God's inexhaustible love. This process is painful, very painful, because the other person has become a true revelation of God's love for you. But the more you are stripped of the God-given support of people, the more you are called to love God for God's sake. This is an awesome and even dreadful love, but it is the love that offers eternal life.

49
Praying for One's Enemies

I find it difficult to conceive of a more concrete way to love than by praying for one's enemies. It makes you conscious of the hard fact that, in God's eyes, you're no more and no less worthy of being loved than any other person, and it creates an awareness of profound solidarity with all other human beings. It creates in you a world-embracing compassion and provides you in increasing measure with a heart free of the compulsive urge to coercion and violence. And you'll be delighted to discover that you can no longer remain angry with people for whom you've really and truly prayed. You will find that you start speaking differently to them or about them, and that you're actually willing to do well to those who've offended you in some way.

50
Anger's Burden

Gradually my inner voice made me see that taking away my burden [of anger] would be like taking away the boat from the fisherman, the keys from the janitor, the car from the chauffeur, or the bricks from the builder. Who would I be without my anger? Who would I be without anyone to judge or condemn? Who would I be without complaints, without feelings of rejection, yes, without enemies? I am the victim, the one who cannot survive without my burden. My burden is my showcase, my bag of tricks, the instrument of my magic, yes, my identity card.

… I slowly rose from my bed soaked in sweat. I stripped, turned on the shower, and let the water pour over my body. "I am a sixty-year-old man," I thought. "What am I going to do with the ten, twenty, or thirty years that are left to me? If I die an angry man shackled to the burden of my past, I will be too heavy for the resurrection!…"

I wrapped myself in a large towel and walked back to my room. I knew I had to choose between clinging to my anger and being sure of death, or cutting my heavy load of angry judgments and trusting that I would not vanish into nothingness. Very deep in me I knew that there would be arms to catch me.

Photo courtesy of the Henri Nouwen Literary Centre

51
Regarding Anger: The Abbot Suggests

First: Allow your angry feelings to come to your awareness and have a careful look at them. Don't deny or suppress them, but let them teach you.

Second: Do not hesitate to talk about angry feelings even when they are related to very small or seemingly insignificant issues. When you don't deal with anger on small issues, how will you ever be ready to deal with it in a real crisis?

Third: Your anger can have good reasons. Talk to me ([Abbot] John Eudes) about it. Maybe I made the wrong decision, maybe I have to change my mind. If I feel that your anger is unrealistic or disproportionate, then we can have a closer look at what made you respond so strongly.

Fourth: Part of the problem might be generalization. A disagreement with a decision, an idea, or event might make you angry at me, the community, the whole country, etc.

Fifth: On a deeper level you might wonder how much of your anger has to do with ego inflation. Anger often reveals how you feel and think about yourself and how important you have made your own ideas and insight. When God becomes again the center and when you can put yourself with all your weaknesses in front of him, you might be able to take some distance and allow your anger to ebb away.

52
Try to Return to the Solid Place

When suddenly you seem to lose all you thought you had gained, do not despair. Your healing is not a straight line. You must expect setbacks and regressions. Don't say to yourself, "All is lost. I have to start all over again." This is not true. What you have gained, you have gained.

Sometimes little things build up and make you lose ground for a moment. Fatigue, a seemingly cold remark, someone's inability to hear you, someone's innocent forgetfulness, which feels like rejection—when all these come together, they can make you feel as if you are right back where you started. But try to think about it instead as being pulled off the road for a while. When you return to the road, you return to the place where you left it, not to where you started.

It is important not to dwell on the small moments when you feel pulled away from your progress. Try to return home, to the solid place within you, immediately. Otherwise, these moments start connecting with similar moments, and together they become powerful enough to pull you far away from the road. Try to remain alert to seemingly innocuous distractions. It is easier to return to the road when you are on the shoulder than when you are pulled all the way into a nearby swamp.

53
Receiving the Water of God's Grace

The Kyrie Eleison—Lord, have mercy—must emerge from a contrite heart. In contrast to a hardened heart, a contrite heart is a heart that does not blame but acknowledges its own part in the sinfulness of the world and so has been made ready to receive God's mercy.

I still remember an evening meditation on Dutch television during which the speaker poured water on hard, dried-out soil, saying, "Look, the soil cannot receive the water and no seed can grow." Then, after crumbling the soil with his hands and pouring water on it again, he said, "It is only the broken soil that can receive the water and make the seed grow and bear fruit."

After seeing this I understood what it meant to begin the Eucharist with a contrite heart, a heart broken open, to receive the water of God's grace.

But how is it possible to begin a thanksgiving celebration with a broken heart? Don't the acknowledgment of our sinful condition and the awareness of our co-responsibility for the evil in the world paralyze us? Isn't a true confession of sins too debilitating? Yes, it is! But no sin can be faced without some knowledge of grace. No loss can be mourned without some intuition that we will find new life.

54
How Will We Remember?

André Malraux remarks in his *Anti-Memoirs* that one day we will realize that we are distinguished as much from each other by the forms our memories take as by our characters. I am wondering what form my memory is taking. It seems that this depends a great deal on myself. I have little to say about events, good or bad, creative or destructive, but much about the way I remember them—that is, the way I start giving them form in the story of my life. I am starting to see how important this is in my day-to-day living. I often say to myself, "How will I remember this day, this disappointment, this conflict, this misunderstanding, this sense of accomplishment, joy, and satisfaction? How will they function in my ongoing task of self-interpretation?"

55
Molding Interruptions

While visiting the University of Notre Dame, where I had been a teacher for a few years, I met an older experienced professor who had spent most of his life there. And while we strolled over the beautiful campus, he said with a certain melancholy in his voice, "You know,… my whole life I have been complaining that my work was constantly interrupted, until I discovered that my interruptions were my work."

What if our interruptions are in fact our opportunities, if they are challenges to an inner response by which growth takes place and through which we come to the fullness of being? What if the events of our history are molding us as a sculptor molds his clay, and if it is only in a careful obedience to these molding hands that we can discover our real vocation and become mature people? What if all the unexpected interruptions are in fact the invitations to give up old-fashioned and out-moded styles of living and are opening up new unexplored areas of experience? And finally: What if our history does not prove to be a blind impersonal sequence of events over which we have no control, but rather reveals to us a guiding hand pointing to a personal encounter in which all our hopes and aspirations will reach their fulfillment?

56
Why Do We Bypass Each Other?

Why is it that we keep that great gift of care so deeply hidden? Why is it that we keep giving dimes without daring to look into the face of the beggar? Why is it that we do not join the lonely eater in the dining hall but look for those we know so well? Why is it that we so seldom knock on a door or grab a phone, just to say hello, just to show that we have been thinking about each other? Why are smiles still hard to get and words of comfort so difficult to come by? Why is it so hard to express thanks to a teacher, admiration to a student, and appreciation to the men and women who cook, clean, and garden? Why do we keep bypassing each other always on the way to something or someone more important?

Maybe simply because we ourselves are so concerned to be different from the others that we do not even allow ourselves to lay down our heavy armor and come together in a mutual vulnerability. Maybe we are so full of our own opinions, ideas and convictions that we have no space left to listen to the other and learn from him or her.

57
The Temptation of Extorting Love

The tragic thing, though, is that we humans aren't capable of dispelling one another's loneliness and lack of self-respect. We humans haven't the wherewithal to relieve one another's most radical predicament. Our ability to satisfy one another's deepest longing is so limited that time and time again we are in danger of disappointing one another. Despite all this, at times our longing can be so intense that it blinds us to our mutual limitations and we are led into the temptation of extorting love, even when reason tells us that we can't give one another any total, unlimited, unconditional love. It is then that love becomes violent. It is then that kisses become bites, caresses become blows, forgiving looks become suspicious glances, lending a sympathetic ear becomes eavesdropping, and heartfelt surrender becomes violation. The borderline between love and force is frequently transgressed, and in our anxiety-ridden times it doesn't take very much to let our desire for love lead us to violent behavior.

58
Becoming People Who "Sound Through"

Our great task is to prevent our fears from boxing our fellow human beings into characterizations and to see them as persons. The word "person" comes from *per-sonare,* which means "sounding through." Our vocation in life is to be and increasingly become persons who "sound through" to each other a greater reality than we ourselves fully know. As persons we sound through a love greater than we ourselves can grasp, a truth deeper than we ourselves can articulate, and a beauty richer than we ourselves can contain. As persons we are called to be transparent to each other, to point far beyond our character to him who has given us his love, truth, and beauty.

When someone says to you, "I love you," or "I am deeply moved by you," or "I am grateful to you," you easily become defensive and wonder what is so special about you. You say or think "Aren't there many other people who are much more lovable or much more intelligent than I am?" But then you have forgotten that you are a person who sounds through to others something much greater and deeper than you yourself can hear.

59
The Garden Is Meant for All

Compassion is daring to acknowledge our mutual destiny so that we might move forward all together into the land which God is showing us. Compassion also means sharing another's joy which can be just as difficult as suffering with him. To give another the chance to be completely happy and to let his joy blossom to the full. Often you can do nothing more than present a bleached smile and say with some effort, "That's really good for you," or "I'm glad to see you made it."

But this compassion is more than a shared slavery with the same fear and same sighs of relief, and more than a shared joy. For if your compassion is born of prayer, it is born of your meeting with God who is also the God of all people. At the moment when you grant that God is God who wants to be your God, and when you give him access to yourself, you realize that a new way has been opened for the person who is beside you. He too has no reason to fear, he too does not have to hide behind a hedge, he too needs no weapons to be a man. The garden which has been unattended for so long is also meant for him.

60
Fear of Dying Alone

You are so afraid of dying alone. Your deeply hidden memories of a fearful birth make you suspect that your death will be equally fearful. You want to be sure that you won't cling to your present existence but will have the inner freedom to let go and trust that something new will be given to you. You know that only someone who truly loves you can help you link this life with the next.

But maybe the death you fear is not simply the death at the end of your present life. Maybe the death at the end of your life won't be so fearful if you can die well now. Yes, the real death—the passage from time into eternity, from the transient beauty of this world to the lasting beauty of the next, from darkness into light—has to be made now. And you do not have to make it alone.

61
Willing to Suffer My Loneliness

I feel very powerless. I want to do something. I have to do something. I have, at least, to speak out against the violence and malnutrition, the oppression and exploitation. Beyond this, I have to act in any way possible to alleviate the pain I see. But there is an even harder task: to carry my own cross, the cross of loneliness and isolation, the cross of the rejections I experience, the cross of my depression and inner anguish. As long as I agonize over the pain of others far away but cannot carry the pain that is uniquely mine, I may become an activist, even a defender of humanity, but not yet a follower of Jesus. Somehow my bond with those who suffer oppression is made real through my willingness to suffer my loneliness. It is a burden I try to avoid, sometimes, by worrying about others. But Jesus says: "Come to me, all you who labor and are overburdened, and I will give you rest" (Mt 11:28). I might think that there is an unbridgeable gap between myself and the Guatemalan wood carrier. But Jesus carried his cross for both of us. We belong together. We must each take up our own cross and follow him, and so discover that we are truly brothers who learn from him who is humble and gentle of heart.

62
The Way to the Heart

Small signs of friendliness can create much joy, and small disturbances between people much sadness, while the "great events" of the day often do not touch us so deeply. An unexpected note from a friend or the passing remark from a neighbor can make or break my day emotionally, while inflation and recession, war and oppression do not touch my emotions directly. A distant catastrophe has less effect than a nearby mishap, and an interpersonal tiff raises more hackles than a world-wide calamity....

But how little do we use this knowledge? What is easier than writing a thank-you note, than sending a card "just to say hello," or to give a call "just to see how things have been." But how seldom do I do this? Still, I realize that every time someone says, "I liked your talk" or "I appreciated your remark" or "Your note really helped" or "You really seem to feel at home here"—I feel my inner life being lifted up and the day seems brighter, the grass greener, and the snow whiter than before. Indeed, the great mystery is that a small, often quite immaterial gesture can change my heart so much. The way to the heart always seems to be a quiet, gentle way.

63
The Healing Power of Children

The children always challenge me to live in the present. They want me to be with them here and now, and they find it hard to understand that I might have other things to do or to think about. After all my experiences with psychotherapy, I suddenly have discovered the great healing power of children. Every time Pablito, Johnny, and Maria run up to welcome me, pick up my suitcase, and bring me to my "roof-room," I marvel at their ability to be fully present to me. Their uninhibited expression of affection and their willingness to receive it pull me directly into the moment and invite me to celebrate life where it is found. Whereas in the past coming home meant time to study, to write letters, and to prepare for classes, it now first of all means time to play....

I now realize that only when I can enter with the children into their joy will I be able to enter also with them into their poverty and pain. God obviously wants me to walk into the world of suffering with a little child on each hand.

64
The Rewards of Compassion

One of the most memorable times of my own life was the time I spent living with the Osco Moreno family in Pamplona Alta near Lima, Peru.... I went to Peru with a deep desire to help the poor. I returned home with a deep gratitude for what I had received. Later, while teaching at Harvard Divinity School, I often felt a real homesickness for "my family." I missed the children hanging onto my arms and legs, laughing loudly and sharing their cookies and drinks with me. I missed the spontaneity, the intimacy, and the generosity with which the poor of Pamplona Alta surrounded me. They literally showered me with gifts of love. No doubt, they were happy and even proud to have this tall "Gringo Padre" with them, but whatever I gave them, it was nothing compared to what I received.

The rewards of compassion are not things to wait for. They are hidden in compassion itself.

65
The Challenge of the Gospel

Perhaps the challenge of the gospel lies precisely in the invitation to accept a gift for which we can give nothing in return. For the gift is the life breath of God, the Spirit who is poured out on us through Jesus Christ. This life breath frees us from fear and gives us new room to live. The person who prayerfully goes about his life is constantly ready to receive the breath of God, and to let his life be renewed and expanded. One who never prays, on the contrary, is like the child with asthma; because he is short of breath, the whole world shrivels up before him. He creeps in a corner gasping for air, and is virtually in agony. But the person who prays opens himself to God and can freely breathe again. He stands upright, stretches out his hands and comes out of his corner, free to boldly stride through the world because he can move about without fear.

A person who prays is one who can once more breathe freely, who has the freedom to move where he wishes with no fears to haunt him.

66
The Prayer of Little Faith

The prayer of little faith is where you hold fast to the concrete of the present situation in order to win a certain security. The prayer of little faith is filled with wishes which beg for immediate fulfillment. This prayer of wish fulfillment has a Santa Claus naiveté which wants to satisfy specific desires....

With the prayer of little faith, it is the concreteness of the wishes which eliminates the possibility for hope. In this prayer, you want to be certain about what is uncertain and you start thinking in terms of one bird in the hand is better than two or ten birds still in the bush. With this prayer, the petition is aimed at getting what you ask for, any way you can, instead of being directed toward the person who might or might not be able to make that wish come true. The person of little faith prays like a child who wants a present from Santa Claus, but who becomes frightened and runs away as soon as he gets his hands on the package. He would rather have nothing more to do with the old bearded gentleman. All the attention is on the gift and none on the one who gives it.

67
In Solitude We Can . . .

In solitude we can slowly unmask the illusion of our possessiveness and discover in the center of our own self that we are not what we can conquer, but what is given to us. In solitude we can listen to the voice of him who spoke to us before we could speak a word, who healed us before we could make any gesture to help, who set us free long before we could free others, and who loved us long before we could give love to anyone. It is in this solitude that we discover that being is more important than having, and that we are worth more than the result of our efforts. In solitude we discover that our life is not a possession to be defended, but a gift to be shared. It's there we recognize that the healing words we speak are not just our own, but are given to us; that the love we can express is part of a greater love; and that the new life we bring forth is not a property to cling to, but a gift to be received.

68
Converting the Silence

One of our main problems is that in this chatty society, silence has become a very fearful thing. For most people, silence creates itchiness and nervousness. Many experience silence not as full and rich, but as empty and hollow. For them silence is like a gaping abyss which can swallow them up. As soon as a minister says during a worship service, "Let us be silent for a few moments," people tend to become restless and preoccupied with only one thought: "When will this be over?" Imposed silence often creates hostility and resentment. Many ministers who have experimented with silence in their services have soon found out that silence can be more demonic than divine and have quickly picked up the signals that were saying: "Please keep talking." It is quite understandable that most forms of ministry avoid silence precisely so as to ward off the anxiety it provokes.

But isn't the purpose of all ministry to reveal that God is not a God of fear but a God of love? And couldn't this be accomplished by gently and carefully converting the empty silence into a full silence, the anxious silence into a peaceful silence, and the restless silence into a restful silence, so that in this converted silence a real encounter with the loving Father could take place?

69
Seeing into the Center

Contemplative life is a human response to the fundamental fact that the central things in life, although spiritually perceptible, remain invisible in large measure and can very easily be overlooked by the inattentive, busy, distracted person that each of us can so readily become. The contemplative looks not so much around things but through them into their center. Through their center he discovers the world of spiritual beauty that is more real, has more density, more mass, more energy, and greater intensity than physical matter. In effect, the beauty of physical matter is a reflection of its inner content. Contemplation is a response to a world that is built in this fashion. That is why the Greek fathers, who were great contemplatives, are known as the dioretic fathers. *Diorao* means to see into, to see through. In celebrating the feast of Corpus Christi, the body of Christ, we celebrate the presence of the risen Christ among us, at the center of our lives, at the center of our very being, at the heart of our community, at the heart of the creation.

70
When the Word Strikes the Heart

Most people who listen to a sermon keep their eyes directed toward the preacher, and rightly so, because he or she asks for attention to the word that is being spoken. But is it also possible for the word to be spoken in such a way that it slowly moves attention away from the pulpit to the heart of the listener and reveals there an inner silence in which it is safe to dwell.

The simple words "The Lord is my shepherd" can be spoken quietly and persistently in such a way that they become like a hedge around a garden in which God's shepherding can be sensed. These words, which at first might seem to be no more than an interesting metaphor, can slowly descend from the mind into the heart. There they may offer the context in which an inner transformation, by the God who transcends all human words and concepts, can take place. Thus, the words "The Lord is my shepherd" lead to the silent pastures where we can dwell in the loving presence of him in whose Name the preacher speaks.

71
The Word's Work

The Word of God is sacramental. That means it is sacred, and as a sacred word it makes present what it indicates.... When we say that God's word is sacred, we mean that God's word is full of God's presence. On the road to Emmaus, Jesus became present through his word, and it was that presence that transformed sadness to joy and mourning to dancing. This is what happens in every Eucharist. The word that is read and spoken wants to lead us into God's presence and transform our hearts and minds. Often we think about the word as an exhortation to go out and change our lives. But the full power of the word lies, not in how we apply it to our lives after we have heard it, but in its transforming power that does its divine work as we listen.

72
The Immediacy of the Word

The Word of God is not a word to apply in our daily lives at some later date; it is a word to heal us through, and in, our listening here and now.

The questions therefore are: How does God come to me as I listen to the word? Where do I discern the healing hand of God touching me through the word? How are my sadness, my grief, and my mourning being transformed at this very moment? Do I sense the fire of God's love purifying my heart and giving me new life? These questions lead me to the sacrament of the word, the sacred place of God's real presence.

At first this might sound quite new for a person living in a society in which the main value of the word is its applicability. But most of us know already, generally unconsciously, of the healing and destroying power of the spoken word. When someone says to me, "I love you," or "I hate you," I am not just receiving some useful information....

When Jesus joins us on the road and explains the scriptures to us, we must listen with our whole being, trusting that the word that created us will also heal us. God wants to become present to us and thus radically transform our fearful hearts.

73
The Ladder of Repetition

The quiet repetition of a single word can help us to descend with the mind into the heart. This repetition has nothing to do with magic. It is not meant to throw a spell on God or to force him into hearing us. On the contrary, a word or sentence repeated frequently can help us to concentrate, to move to the center, to create an inner stillness and thus to listen to the voice of God. When we simply try to sit silently and wait for God to speak to us, we find ourselves bombarded with endless conflicting thoughts and ideas. But when we use a very simple sentence such as "O God, come to my assistance," or "Jesus, master, have mercy on me," or a word such as "Lord" or "Jesus," it is easier to let the many distractions pass by without being misled by them. Such a simple, easily repeated prayer can slowly empty out our crowded interior life and create the quiet space where we can dwell with God. It can be like a ladder along which we can descend into the heart and ascend to God. Our choice of words depends on our needs and the circumstances of the moment, but it is best to use words from Scripture.

74
Imagination and Prayer

Prayer also has much to do with imagining. When I bring myself into the presence of God, I imagine him in many ways: as a loving father, a supporting sister, a caring mother, a severe teacher, an honest judge, a fellow traveler, an intimate friend, a gentle healer, a challenging leader, a demanding taskmaster. All these "personalities" create images in my mind that affect not only what I think, but also how I actually experience myself. I believe that true prayer makes us into what we imagine. To pray to God leads to becoming like God.

When Saint Ignatius proposes that we use all our senses in our meditation, he does more than offer a technique to help us concentrate on the mysteries of God's revelation. He wants us to imagine the reality of the divine as fully as possible so that we can slowly be divinized by that reality. Divinization is, indeed, the goal of all prayer and meditation. This divinization allows St. Paul to say: "I live now not with my own life but with the life of Christ who lives in me" (Gal 2:20).

75
The Value of Memorized Prayers

One simple and somewhat obvious technique is memorization. The expression "to know by heart" already suggests its value. Personally I regret the fact that I know so few prayers and psalms by heart. Often I need a book to pray, and without one I tend to fall back on the poor spontaneous creations of my mind. Part of the reason, I think, that it is so hard to pray "without ceasing" is that few prayers are available to me outside church settings. Yet I believe that prayers which I know by heart could carry me through very painful crises. The Methodist minister Fred Morris told me how Psalm 23 ("The Lord is my shepherd") had carried him through the gruesome hours in the Brazilian torture chamber and had given him peace in his darkest hour. And I keep wondering which words I can take with me in the hour when I have to survive without books. I fear that in crisis situations I will have to depend on my own unredeemed ramblings and not have the Word of God to guide me.

76
Prayer as Ministry

Jesus continuously left his apostles to enter into prayer with the Father. The more I read the Gospels, the more I am struck with Jesus' single-minded concern with the Father. From the day his parents found him in the Temple, Jesus speaks about his Father as the source of all his words and actions. When he withdraws himself from the crowd and even from his closest friends, he withdraws to be with the Father. [See Mk 1:35.] All through his life Jesus considers his relationship with the Father as the center, beginning, and end of his ministry. All he says and does he says and does in the name of the Father. He comes from the Father and returns to the Father, and it is in his Father's house that he wants to prepare a place for us.

It is obvious that Jesus does not maintain his relationship with the Father as a means of fulfilling his ministry. On the contrary, his relationship with the Father is the core of his ministry. Therefore, prayer, days alone with God, or moments of silence, should never be seen or understood as healthy devices to keep in shape, to charge our "spiritual batteries," or to build up energy for ministry. No, they are all ministry.

77
Who Takes the Credit?

With many others, I wanted to become a self-sufficient star. And most of my fellow intellectuals joined me in that desire.

But all of us highly trained individuals are facing today a world on the brink of total destruction. And now we start to wonder how we might join forces to make peace! What kind of peace can this possibly be? Who can paint a portrait of people who all want to take the center seat? Who can build a beautiful church with people who are interested only in erecting the tower? Who can bake a birthday cake with people who want only to put the candles on? You all know the problem. When all want the honor of being the final peacemaker, there never will be peace.

78
Let Me Not Run Away

Dear Lord, your disciple Peter wanted to know who would betray you. You pointed to Judas but a little later also to him. Judas betrayed, Peter denied you. Judas hanged himself, Peter became the apostle whom you made the first among equals. Lord, give me faith, faith in your endless mercy, your boundless forgiveness, your unfathomable goodness. Let me not be tempted to think that my sins are too great to be forgiven, too abominable to be touched by your mercy. Let me never run away from you but return to you again and again, asking you to be my Lord, my Shepherd, my Stronghold, and my Refuge. Take me under your wing, O Lord, and let me know that you do not reject me as long as I keep asking you to forgive me. Perhaps my doubt in your forgiveness is a greater sin than the sins I consider too great to be forgiven. Perhaps I make myself too important, too great when I think that I cannot be embraced by you anymore. Lord, look at me, accept my prayer as you accepted Peter's prayer, and let me not run away from you in the night as Judas did.

79
The Mystery of the Descending Way

It is so difficult to express the richness of the gospel. I would really like to write down every saying of Jesus because again and again, each time in a different way, he presents to us the great mystery of the descending way. It is the way of suffering, but also the way to healing. It is the way of humiliation, but also the way to resurrection. It is the way of tears, but of tears that turn into tears of joy. It is the way of hiddenness, but also the way that leads to the light that will shine for all people. It is the way of persecution, oppression, martyrdom, and death, but also the way to the full disclosure of God's love. In the gospel of John, Jesus says: "As Moses lifted up the snake in the desert, so must the Son of man be lifted up." You see in these words how the descending way of Jesus becomes the ascending way. The "lifting up" that Jesus speaks of refers both to his being raised up on the cross in total humiliation and to his being raised up from the dead in total glorification.

80
Free Me from My Dark Past

Dear Lord, free me from my dark past, into which I often feel myself falling as if into a deep cistern. You are the light that has come into the world so that whoever believes in you need not stay in darkness any longer. Do not allow me to sink back into my own dark pit, O Lord, but let your warm, gentle, life-giving light lift me from my grave. Vincent van Gogh painted you as the sun when he painted the resurrection of Lazarus. In so doing, he wanted to express his own liberation from a dark, imprisoning past. Lord, keep showing me your light, and give me the strength to rise and follow you without ever looking back. You are my Strength, my Refuge, and my Stronghold. As long as I keep my eyes on you, there is no reason to return to past events, past patterns, past ideas. In your light all becomes new. Let me be fully yours. Amen.

81
Awaiting the Second Advent

John Eudes [Abbot] said ... that we should desire not only the first coming of Christ in his lowly human gentleness but also his second coming as the judge of our lives. I sensed that the desire for Christ's judgment is a real aspect of holiness and realized how little that desire was mine.

In his Advent sermon, Guerric of Igny understands that it is not easy to desire with fervor this second coming. Therefore, he says that if we cannot prepare ourselves for the day of judgment by desire, let us at least prepare ourselves by fear. Now I see better how part of Christian maturation is the slow but persistent deepening of fear to the point where it becomes desire. The fear of God is not in contrast with his mercy. Therefore, words such as fear and desire, justice and mercy have to be relearned and reunderstood when we use them in our intimate relationship with the Lord.

82
The Idolatry of Our Dreams

When we feel like a small child during the day, our frustrated mind is all too willing to make us into tall and great heroes in our dreaming moments: into victorious heroes admired by all those who do not take us so seriously when we are awake, or into tragic heroes recognized too late by those who criticized us during our life. In our dreams, we can become like the first Joseph generously forgiving his brother in Egypt or, like the second one, carefully carrying his persecuted child to the same land. In our dreams, we can freely erect statues to honor our own martyrdom and burn incense for our wounded self. These images with which we often fill our unfulfilled desires remind us how quickly we substitute one idol for another. Unmasking illusions twenty-four hours a day is harder than we might think.

It would be unwise to try to change our dreams directly or to start worrying about the unexpected images that appear during our nights. The idols of our dreams, however, are humbling reminders that we still have a long way to go before we are ready to meet our God, not the God created by our own hands or mind, but the uncreated God out of whose loving hands we are born.

83
Touching the Child Within

I know that I am a child, a child who, underneath all my accomplishments and successes, keeps crying out to be held safe and loved without conditions. I also know that losing touch with my child is losing touch with Jesus and all who belong to him. Each time I touch my own child, I touch my powerlessness and my fear of being left alone with no one to give me a safe place.

Jesus falls beneath the cross to allow me to reclaim my child, that place in me where I am out of control and in desperate need of being lifted up and reassured. The abandoned children of the world are in me. Jesus tells me not to be afraid, to face them in my heart and suffer with them. He wants me to discover that beyond all emotions of rejection and abandonment there is love, real love, lasting love, love that comes from a God who became flesh and who will never leave his children alone.

84
Jesus Meets His Mother

Jesus met his mother as he was being led to his execution. Mary did not faint; she did not scream in rage or despair; she did not try to prevent the soldiers from torturing him more. She looked him in the eyes and knew that this was his hour. In Cana, when she had asked his help, he had put some distance between them and said: "Woman,... My hour has not yet come" (Jn 2:4). But now his sorrow and her sorrow merged in a deep knowledge of the hour in which God's plan of salvation was being fulfilled. Soon Mary will stand under the cross and Jesus will give her to John, his beloved disciple, with the words: "This is your mother" (Jn 19:27). Mary's sorrow has made her not only the mother of Jesus, but also the mother of all her suffering children. She stood under the cross; she stands there still and looks into the eyes of those who are tempted to respond to their pain with revenge, retaliation, or despair. Her sorrow has made her heart a heart that embraces all her children, wherever they may be, and offers them maternal consolation and comfort.

85
Our Tears Reveal...

Weeping and mourning are considered by many people as signs of weakness. They say that crying will not help anybody. Only action is needed. And still, Jesus wept over Jerusalem; he wept also when he heard that his friend Lazarus had died. Our tears reveal to us the painful human condition of brokenness; they connect us deeply with the inevitability of human suffering; they offer the gentle context for compassionate action. If we cannot confess our own limitations, sin, and mortality, then our well-intended actions for the making of a better world easily backfire on us and become expressions of an undirected anger and frustration. Our tears can lead us to the heart of Jesus who wept for our world. As we weep with him, we are led to his heart and discover there the most authentic response to our losses. The tears shed by the women of Nicaragua and the millions who mourn their dead throughout the world, can make our soil rich with the fruits of compassion, forgiveness, gentleness, and healing action. We, too, must weep and so become more and more humble people.

86
A Look at the Human Hand

A hand waits for the touch of another hand. The human hand is so mysterious. It can create and destroy, caress and strike, make welcoming gestures and condemning signs; it can bless and curse, heal and wound, beg and give. A hand can become a threatening fist as well as a symbol of safety and protection. It can be most feared and most longed for.

One of the most life-giving images is that of human hands reaching out to each other, touching each other, interconnecting and merging into a sign of peace and reconciliation. In contrast, one of the most despairing images is that of a hand stretched open, waiting to be touched with care, while people walk heedlessly by. This is not only an image of the loneliness of the individual person, but of the loneliness of a divided humanity. The hand of the poor world reaches out to be touched by the hand of the rich world, but the preoccupations of the rich prevent them from seeing the poor, and humanity remains broken and fragmented.

87
A Look at God's Hand and Mine

Ever since I came to know God's hand—not as the powerful hand controlling the course of history, but as the powerless hand [of Jesus] asking to be grasped by a caring human hand—I have been looking differently at my own hands. Gradually, I have come to see God's powerless hand reaching out to me from everywhere in the world, and, the clearer I see it, the closer these outstretched hands seem to be. The hands of the poor begging for food, the hands of the lonely calling for simple presence, the hands of the children asking to be lifted up and held, the hands of the sick hoping to be touched, the hands of the unskilled wanting to be trained—all these hands are the hands of the fallen Jesus waiting for others to come and give him their hand.

There is always in me the temptation to think about the begging hands of the people in Calcutta, Cairo, or New York, far, far away, and not to see the open hands reaching out right into my own living space. Every night I go to rest and look at my hands. And I have to ask them: "Did you reach out to one of the open hands around you and bring a little bit of peace, hope, courage, and confidence?"

88
Revolution and Conversion

For a Christian, Jesus is the man in whom it has indeed become manifest that revolution and conversion cannot be separated in man's search for experiential transcendence. His appearance in our midst has made it undeniably clear that changing the human heart and changing human society are not separate tasks, but are as interconnected as the two beams of the cross.

Jesus was a revolutionary, who did not become an extremist, since he did not offer an ideology, but himself. He was also a mystic, who did not use his intimate relationship with God to avoid the social evils of his time, but shocked his milieu to the point of being executed as a rebel. In this sense he also remains for nuclear man the way to liberation and freedom.

Leadership Rooted in Relationship

It is of vital importance to reclaim the mystical aspect of theology so that every word spoken, every advice given, and every strategy developed can come from a heart that knows God intimately. I have the impression that many of the debates within the Church around issues such as the papacy, the ordination of women, the marriage of priests, homosexuality, birth control, abortion, and euthanasia take place on a primarily moral level. On that level, different parties battle about right or wrong. But that battle is often removed from the experience of God's first love which lies at the base of all human relationships. Words like right-wing, reactionary, conservative, liberal, and left-wing are used to describe people's opinions, and many discussions then seem more like political battles for power than spiritual searches for the truth.

Christian leaders cannot simply be persons who have well-informed opinions about the burning issues of our time. Their leadership must be rooted in the permanent, intimate relationship with the incarnate Word, Jesus.

90
Jesus' First Temptation

Jesus' first temptation was to be relevant: to turn stones into bread. Oh, how often have I wished I could do that! Walking through the "young towns" on the outskirts of Lima, Peru, where children die from malnutrition and contaminated water, I would not have been able to reject the magical gift of making the dusty stone-covered streets into places where people could pick up any of the thousands of rocks and discover that they were croissants, coffee cakes, or fresh-baked buns…. Aren't we called to heal the sick, feed the hungry, and alleviate the suffering of the poor? Jesus was faced with these same questions, but when he was asked to prove his power as the Son of God by the relevant behavior of changing stones into bread, he clung to his mission to proclaim the word.

91
Jesus Asks Peter—and Us

The question is not: How many people take you seriously? How much are you going to accomplish? Can you show some results? But: Are you in love with Jesus? Perhaps another way of putting the question would be: Do you know the incarnate God? In our world of loneliness and despair, there is an enormous need for men and women who know the heart of God, a heart that forgives, that cares, that reaches out and wants to heal. In that heart there is no suspicion, no vindictiveness, no resentment, and not a tinge of hatred. It is a heart that wants only to give love and receive love in response. It is a heart that suffers immensely because it sees the magnitude of human pain and the great resistance to trusting the heart of God who wants to offer consolation and hope.

92
Tempted to Replace Love with Power

What makes the temptation of power so seemingly irresistible? Maybe it is that power offers an easy substitute for the hard task of love. It seems easier to be God than to love God, easier to control people than to love people, easier to own life than to love life. Jesus asks, "Do you love me?" We ask, "Can we sit at your right hand and your left hand in your Kingdom?" (Mt 20:21).... We have been tempted to replace love with power. Jesus lived that temptation in the most agonizing way from the desert to the cross. The long painful history of the Church is the history of people ever and again tempted to choose power over love, control over the cross, being a leader over being led. Those who resisted this temptation to the end and thereby give us hope are the true saints.

93
Do Not Search on Your Own

If you yourself are seriously searching for the specific way which you must walk to follow Jesus, then I beg you not to do so on your own, but within a eucharistic community. I feel more and more certain that the way of Jesus can't be found outside the community of those who believe in Jesus and make their belief visible by coming together around the eucharistic table. The Eucharist is the heart and center of being-the-church. Without it there is no people of God, no community of faith, no church. Often enough, you see that people who abandon the church have trouble in holding on to Jesus. This becomes understandable when you consider that the church is the eucharistic community in which Jesus gives us his body and blood as gifts that come to us from heaven and help us to find the way of love in our own lives.

94
The Center of My Life

My whole being is rooted in the Eucharist. For me, to be a priest means to be ordained to present Christ every day as food and drink to my fellow Christians. I sometimes wonder if those who are close to me are sufficiently aware of the fact that the Eucharist constitutes the core of my life. I do so many other things and have so many secondary identities—teacher, speaker, and writer—that it is easy to consider the Eucharist as the least important part of my life. But the opposite is true. The Eucharist is the center of my life and everything else receives its meaning from that center. I am saying this with so much emphasis in the hope that you will understand what I mean when I say that my life must be a continuing proclamation of the death and resurrection of Christ. It is first and foremost through the Eucharist that this proclamation takes place.

95
Do We Invite Jesus In?

It is one of the characteristics of our contemporary society that encounters, good as they may be, don't become deep relationships. Thus our life is filled with good advice, helpful ideas, wonderful perspectives, but they are simply added to the many other ideas and perspectives and so leave us "uncommitted." In a society with such an informational overload, even the most significant encounters can be reduced to "something interesting" among many other interesting things.

Only with an invitation to "come and stay with me" can an interesting encounter develop into a transforming relationship.

One of the most decisive moments of the Eucharist—and of our life—is the moment of invitation. Do we say: "It was wonderful to meet you, thank you for your insights, your advice, and your encouragement. I hope the rest of your journey goes well. Goodbye!" Or do we say: "I have heard you, my heart is changing ... please come into my home and see where and how I live!" This invitation to come and see is the invitation that makes all the difference.

Jesus is a very interesting person; his words are full of wisdom. His presence is heart-warming. His gentleness and kindness are deeply moving. His message is very challenging. But do we invite him into our home?

96
As If I Were Resisting the Love

Lord, you kneel before me; you hold my naked feet in your hands, and you look up at me and smile. Within me I feel the protest arising, "No, Lord, you shall never wash my feet." It is as if I were resisting the love you offer me. I want to say, "You don't really know me, my dark feelings, my pride, my lust, my greed. I may speak the right words, but my heart is so far from you. No, I am not good enough to belong to you. You must have someone else in mind, not me." But you look at me with utter tenderness, saying, "I want you to be with me. I want you to have a full share in my life. I want you to belong to me as much as I belong to my Father. I want to wash you completely clean so that you and I can be one and so that you can do to others what I have done to you." I have to let go of all my fears, distrust, doubts and anguish and simply let you wash me clean and make me your friend whom you love with a love that has no bounds.

97
We Will Taste the Joy

"Can you drink the cup that I am going to drink?" When Jesus brought this question to John and James, and when they impulsively answered with a big "We can," he made this terrifying, yet hope-filled prediction: "Very well; you shall drink my cup." The cup of Jesus would be their cup. What Jesus would live, they would live. Jesus didn't want his friends to suffer, but he knew that for them, as for him, suffering was the only and necessary way to glory. Later he would say to two of his disciples: "Was it not necessary that the Christ should suffer before entering into his glory?" (Lk 24:26). The "cup of sorrows" and the "cup of joys" cannot be separated. Jesus knew this, even though in the midst of his anguish in the garden, when his soul was "sorrowful to the point of death" (Mt 26:38), he needed an angel from heaven to remind him of it. Our cup is often so full of pain that joy seems completely unreachable. When we are crushed like grapes, we cannot think of the wine we will become.... Then we need to be reminded that our cup of sorrow is also our cup of joy and that one day we will be able to taste the joy as fully as we now taste the sorrow.

98
Holding the Cup of Life

Before we drink the cup, we must hold it!...

Holding the cup of life means looking critically at what we are living. This requires great courage, because when we start looking, we might be terrified by what we see. Questions may arise that we don't know how to answer. Doubts may come up about things we thought we were sure about. Fear may emerge from unexpected places. We are tempted to say: "Let's just live life. All this thinking about it only makes things harder." Still, we intuitively know that without looking at life critically we lose our vision and our direction. When we drink the cup without holding it first, we may simply get drunk and wander around aimlessly.

Holding the cup of life is a hard discipline. We are thirsty people who like to start drinking at once. But we need to restrain our impulse to drink, put both of our hands around the cup, and ask ourselves, "What am I given to drink? What is in my cup? Is it safe to drink? Is it good for me? Will it bring me health?"

99
Lifting the Cup of Life

The cup of sorrow and joy, when lifted for others to see and celebrate, becomes a cup of life....

Mostly we are willing to look back at our lives and say: "I am grateful for the *good* things that brought me to this place." But when we lift our cup to life, we must dare to say: "I am grateful for *all* that has happened to me and led me to this moment." This gratitude which embraces all of our past is what makes our life a true gift for others, because this gratitude erases bitterness, resentment, regret, and revenge as well as all jealousies and rivalries. It transforms our past into a fruitful gift for the future, and makes our life, all of it, into a life that gives life.

The enormous individualism of our society, in which so much emphasis is on "doing it yourself," prevents us from lifting our lives for each other. But each time we dare to step beyond our fear, to be vulnerable and lift our cup, our own and other people's lives will blossom in unexpected ways.

100
Drinking the Cup of Life

The cup that we hold and lift we must drink....

The world is full of places to drink: bars, pubs, coffee and tea rooms. Even when we go out to eat, the waiter's first question is always "Can I offer you something to drink?" That is also one of the first questions we ask our guests when they enter our home.

It seems that most of our drinking takes place in a context in which we feel, at least for a moment, at home with ourselves and safe with others. Drinking a cup of coffee to interrupt work for a moment, stopping for tea in the afternoon, having a "quick drink" before dinner, taking a glass of wine before going to bed—all these are moments to say to ourselves or others: "It is good to be alive in the midst of all that is going on, and I want to be reminded of that."

Drinking the cup of life makes our own everything we are living. It is saying, "This is my life," but also "I want this to be my life." Drinking the cup of life is fully appropriating and internalizing our own unique existence, with all its sorrows and joys.

101
Take and Eat, Go and Tell

The Eucharist concludes with a mission. "Go, now and tell!" The Latin words "Ite Missa est," with which the priest used to conclude the Mass, literally mean: "Go, this is your mission."

Communion is not the end. Mission is. Communion, that sacred intimacy with God, is not the final moment of the Eucharistic life. We recognized him, but that recognition is not just for us to savor or to keep as a secret.... "Go and tell." That's the conclusion of the Eucharistic celebration; that too is the final call of the Eucharistic life. "Go and tell. What you have heard and seen is not just for yourself. It is for the brothers and sisters and for all who are ready to receive it. Go, don't linger, don't wait, don't hesitate, but move now and return to the places from which you came, and let those whom you left behind in their hiding places know that there is nothing to be afraid of, that he is risen, risen indeed."

It is important to realize that the mission is, first of all, a mission to those who are no strangers to us. They know us and, like us, have heard about Jesus but have become discouraged. The mission is always first of all to our own, our family, our friends, those who are an intimate part of our lives.

102
The Spirit Manifest Through Many

It is so easy to narrow Jesus down to our Jesus, to our experience of his love, to our way of knowing him. But Jesus left us so as to send his Spirit, and his Spirit blows where it wants. The community of faith is the place where many stories about the way of Jesus are being told. These stories can be very different from each other. They might even seem to conflict. But as we keep listening attentively to the Spirit manifesting itself through many people, in words as well as in silence, through confrontation as well as invitation, in gentleness as well as firmness, with tears as well as smiles—then we can gradually discern that we belong together, as one body knitted together by the Spirit of Jesus.

In the Eucharist we are asked to leave the table and go to our friends to discover with them that Jesus is truly alive and calls us together to become a new people—a people of the resurrection.

103
In the Face of Death (Part 1)

The real struggle was not a matter of leaving loved ones. The real struggle had to do with leaving behind me people whom I had not forgiven and people who had not forgiven me. These feelings kept me bound to the old body and brought me great sadness. I suddenly felt an immense desire to call around my bed all who were angry with me and all with whom I was angry, to embrace them, ask them to forgive me, and offer them my forgiveness. As I thought of them, I realized that they represented a host of opinions, judgments, and even condemnations that had enslaved me to this world. It almost seemed that much of my energy had gone into proving to myself and to others that I was right in my conviction that some people could not be trusted, that others were using me or were trying to push me aside, and that whole groups and categories of people were falling short of the mark. Thus I kept holding on to the illusion that I am destined to be the evaluator and judge of human behavior.

104
In the Face of Death (Part 2)

As I felt life weakening in me, I felt a deep desire to forgive and to be forgiven, to let go of all evaluations and opinions, to be free from the burden of judgments. I said to Sue, "Please tell everyone who has hurt me that I forgive them from my heart, and please ask everyone whom I have hurt to forgive me too." As I said this, I felt I was taking off the wide leather belts that I had worn while chaplain with the rank of captain in the army. Those belts not only girded my waist, but also crossed my chest and shoulders. They had given me prestige and power. They had encouraged me to judge people and put them in their place. Although my stay in the army was very brief, I had, in my mind, never fully removed my belts. But I knew now that I did not want to die with these belts holding me captive.

105
The Gentle Movements of the Spirit

While realizing that ten years ago I didn't have the faintest idea that I would end up where I now am, I still like to keep up the illusion that I am in control of my own life. I like to decide what I most need, what I will do next, what I want to accomplish, and how others will think of me. While being so busy running my own life, I become oblivious to the gentle movements of the Spirit of God within me, pointing me in directions quite different from my own.

It requires a lot of inner solitude and silence to become aware of these divine movements. God does not shout, scream, or push. The Spirit of God is soft and gentle like a small voice or a light breeze. It is the spirit of love.

106
What I Learned About Dying

If I die with much anger and bitterness, I will leave my family and friends behind in confusion, guilt, shame, or weakness. When I felt my death approaching, I suddenly realized how much I could influence the hearts of those whom I would leave behind. If I could truly say that I was grateful for what I had lived, eager to forgive and be forgiven, full of hope that those who loved me would continue their lives in joy and peace, and confident that Jesus who calls me would guide all who somehow had belonged to my life—if I could do that—I would, in the hour of my death, reveal more true spiritual freedom than I had been able to reveal during all the years of my life. I realized on a very deep level that dying is the most important act of living. It involves a choice to bind others with guilt or to set them free with gratitude.

107
A Mission into Time

Even though I often give in to the many fears and warnings of my world, I still believe deeply that our few years on this earth are part of a much larger event that stretches out far beyond the boundaries of our birth and death. I think of it as a mission into time, a mission that is very exhilarating and even exciting, mostly because the One who sent me on the mission is waiting for me to come home and tell the story of what I have learned.

Am I afraid to die? I am every time I let myself be seduced by the noisy voices of my world telling me that my "little life" is all I have and advising me to cling to it with all my might. But when I let these voices move to the background of my life and listen to that small soft voice calling me the Beloved, I know that there is nothing to fear and that dying is the greatest act of love, the act that leads me into the eternal embrace of my God whose love is everlasting.

108
The Past and Future Meet the Present

When Jesus came to redeem mankind, he came to free us from the boundaries of time. Through him it became clear not only that God is with us wherever our presence is in time or space, but also that our past does not have to be forgotten or denied but can be remembered and forgiven, and that we are still waiting for him to come back and reveal to us what remains unseen. When Jesus left his apostles he gave them bread and wine in memory of what he did so that he could stay in their presence until the moment of his return. The word Eucharist, which means thanksgiving, expresses a way of accepting life in which the past and the future are brought together in the present moment. This thanksgiving is meant to be a way of living that makes it possible to really celebrate life. Frequently, this Eucharistic celebration of life takes place elsewhere than where it is formally planned. Life is not always really celebrated where liturgies are held. Sometimes it is, but quite often it is not. Perhaps we have to become more sensitive to people and places where no one ever talks about liturgical reform or changes, but where life is fully affirmed in the deepest Eucharistic sense.

109
Listen to the Book

L isten to the book. By that I mean read the Bible; read books about the Bible, about the spiritual life, and the lives of "great" saints. I know you read a good deal; but a lot of what you read distracts you from the way that Jesus is showing you. The secondary school and university offer you little in the way of "spiritual reading." That's why it's very important for you to read regularly books which will help you in your spiritual life. Many people are brought to God through spiritual literature that they chance or choose to read. Augustine, Ignatius, Thomas Merton, and many others have been converted through the book. The challenge, however, is not to read a "spiritual" book as a source of interesting information, but rather to listen to it as to a voice that addresses you directly. It isn't easy to let a text "read" you. Your thirst for knowledge and information often makes you desire to own the word, instead of letting the word own you. Even so, you will learn the most by listening carefully to the Word that seeks admission to your heart.

110
Choose the Joy

People who have come to know the joy of God do not deny the darkness, but they choose not to live in it. They claim that the light that shines in the darkness can be trusted more than the darkness itself and that a little bit of light can dispel a lot of darkness. They point each other to flashes of light here and there, and remind each other that they reveal the hidden but real presence of God. They discover that there are people who heal each other's wounds, forgive each other's offenses, share their possessions, foster the spirit of community, celebrate the gifts they have received, and live in constant anticipation of the full manifestation of God's glory.

Every moment of each day I have the chance to choose between cynicism and joy. Every thought I have can be cynical or joyful. Every word I speak can be cynical or joyful. Every action can be cynical or joyful. Increasingly I am aware of all these possible choices, and increasingly I discover that every choice for joy in turn reveals more joy and offers more reason to make life a true celebration in the house of the Father.

111
Do Not Be Unbelieving, Believe

Often I act as though you are not visible enough, not audible enough, not tangible enough. The world around me is so easy to see, to hear and to touch, and, before I fully realize it, I am already seeing, hearing and touching with much greed and lust—always asking for more and never fully satisfied. And, as I run away from you, pulled by the colors, sounds and substance of my surroundings, I accuse you for not being concrete enough, and I say what your own disciple Thomas said, "Unless I can put my hands in his side, I refuse to believe."

O, dear Jesus, why can't I simply trust you and the many ways in which you have already shown me your love? Who had the privilege of knowing about you from the moment he could know? I did! Who had parents, friends and teachers radiating your affection and care? I did! Who had so many opportunities to know you better and love you more? I did! And still I remain sulky and unconvinced, saying, "Unless I can put my hands in his side, I refuse to believe."

You are so patient, Lord. You are not angry or resentful. You stand there, take my hand and say, "Put your hand into my side. Do not be unbelieving any more, but believe."

112
Make Me a Real Disciple

Dear Lord, even when I know everything about you, even when I have studied all the Scriptures with care, even when I have a great desire and willpower to work in your service, I can do nothing without the gift of your Spirit. Often I realize that the clearest vision of the true life, and the most sincere wish to live it, is not enough to make me a true disciple. Only when your Spirit has entered into the depth of my being can I be a real Christian, a man who lives in and with and through you.

You made it clear to your friends that they should not leave Jerusalem but should "stay in the city until they are clothed with power from on high."

Lord, I pray for the power of your Spirit. Let this power invade me and transform me into a real disciple, willing to follow you even where I would rather not go. Amen.

Acknowledgments

For all Nouwen selections, we gratefully acknowledge permission, granted as follows:

1. From *A Cry for Mercy* by Henri J. M. Nouwen. © 1981 by Henri J. M. Nouwen. Used by permission of Doubleday, a division of Bantam Doubleday Dell Publishing Group, Inc.

2. From *Can You Drink the Cup?* by Henri J. M. Nouwen. © 1996 by Ave Maria Press, Notre Dame, IN 56556. Used by permission of the publisher.

3. From *Here and Now* by Henri J. M. Nouwen. © 1994 by Henri J. M. Nouwen. Used by permission of The Crossroad Publishing Company, New York.

4. From *The Living Reminder* by Henri J. M. Nouwen. © 1977 by Henri J. M. Nouwen. Reprinted by permission of HarperCollins Publishers, Inc.

5. From *A Cry for Mercy* by Henri J. M. Nouwen. © 1981 by Henri J. M. Nouwen. Used by permission of Doubleday, a division of Bantam Doubleday Dell Publishing Group, Inc.

55. From *Reaching Out* by Henri Nouwen. © 1975 by Henri J. M. Nouwen. Used by permission of Doubleday, a division of Bantam Doubleday Dell Publishing Group, Inc.

56. From *Out of Solitude* by Henri J. M. Nouwen. © 1974 by Ave Maria Press, Notre Dame, IN 56556. Used by permission of the publisher.

57. From *Letters to Marc about Jesus* by Henri J. M. Nouwen. © 1987, 1988 by Harper & Row, Publishers, Inc. and Darton, Longman & Todd, Ltd. Reprinted by permission of HarperCollins Publishers, Inc.

58. From *Clowning in Rome* by Henri J. M. Nouwen. © 1979 by Henri J. M. Nouwen. Used by permission of Doubleday, a division of Bantam Doubleday Dell Publishing Group, Inc.

59. From *With Open Hands* by Henri J. M. Nouwen. © 1972 by Ave Maria Press, Notre Dame, IN 56556. Used by permission of the publisher.

60. From *The Inner Voice of Love* by Henri Nouwen. © 1996 by Henri Nouwen. Used by permission of Doubleday, a division of Bantam Doubleday Dell Publishing Group, Inc.

61. From *Walk with Jesus* by Henri Nouwen. © 1990 by Henri Nouwen. Used by permission of Orbis Books.

93. From *Letters to Marc about Jesus* by Henri J. M. Nouwen. © 1987, 1988 by Harper & Row, Publishers, Inc. and Darton, Longman & Todd, Ltd. Reprinted by permission of HarperCollins Publishers, Inc.

94. From *A Letter of Consolation* by Henri J. M. Nouwen. © 1982 by Henri J. M. Nouwen. Reprinted by permission of HarperCollins Publishers, Inc.

95. From *With Burning Hearts* by Henri J. M. Nouwen. © 1994 by Henri J. M. Nouwen. Used by permission of Orbis Books.

96. From *Heart Speaks to Heart* by Henri J. M. Nouwen. © 1989 by Ave Maria Press, Notre Dame, IN 56556. Used by permission of the publisher.

97-100. From *Can You Drink the Cup?* by Henri J. M. Nouwen. © 1996 by Ave Maria Press, Notre Dame, IN 56556. Used by permission of the publisher.

101-102. From *With Burning Hearts* by Henri J. M. Nouwen. © 1994 by Henri J. M. Nouwen. Used by permission of Orbis Books.

103-104. From *Beyond the Mirror* by Henri J. M. Nouwen. © 1990 by Henri J. M. Nouwen. Used with permission of The Crossroad Publishing Company, New York.

105. From *Here and Now* by Henri J. M. Nouwen. © 1994 by Henri J. M. Nouwen. Used by permission of The Crossroad Publishing Company, New York.